PLASTIC

ECO Activities

Written by
Louise Nelson

CRABTREE
PUBLISHING COMPANY
WWW.CRABTREEBOOKS.COM

CRABTREE
PUBLISHING COMPANY
WWW.CRABTREEBOOKS.COM

Author: Louise Nelson

Editorial Director: Kathy Middleton

Editors: Robin Twiddy, Ellen Rodger

Proofreader: Crystal Sikkens

Cover/Interior Design: Jasmine Pointer

Production coordinator and
 Prepress technician: Margaret Amy Salter

Print coordinator: Katherine Berti

Photo Credits

All images are courtesy of Shutterstock.com, unless otherwise specified. With thanks to Getty Images, Thinkstock Photo and iStockphoto.bPaper Texture Throughout – Borja Andreu. Front Cover – chuchiko17, 826A IA, KittyVector, elenabsl, Alrandir, sundora14, AlenKadr. 4 – TinnaPong. 5 – Vytas999, Phovoir, Marlon Trottmann, Nastelbo. 6–7 – Janis Smits, MvanCaspel, HeinzTeh, mkos83, Alba_alioth. 8–9 – ESB Professional, Yury Kosourov, Dmitry Kolmakov, IB Photography, Stock Up, Elena Polovinko, SweetLemons, Marija Stepanovic, riphoto3, monticello, Dan Kosmayer, Anton Starikov. 10–11 – peart,ABB Photo, Lee Yiu Tung, Africa Studio, Bushidoh. 12–13 – Wutthichai Phosri, pikselstock, Liliya Krasnova, Becky Starsmore, andregric, BorisShevchuk, Ayrat Gabdrakhmanov, SmileStudio. 14–15 –Wutthichai Phosri, Porstocker. 16–17 – Pixel-Shot, Papakah. 18–19 – chuchiko17, BW Folsom, AlexussK, kak2s, nikkytok. 20–21 – chuchiko17, elenabsl. 22–23 –Vitaliya.

Library and Achives Canada Cataloguing in Publication

Title: Plastic : eco activities / written byLouise Nelson.
Names: Nelson, Louise, 1981- author.
Description: Includes index.
Identifiers: Canadiana (print) 2020035681X | Canadiana (ebook) 20200356828
  ISBN 9781427128621 (hardcover) |
  ISBN 9781427128669 (softcover) |
  ISBN 9781427128706 (HTML)
Subjects: LCSH: Plastics craft—Juvenile literature. | LCSH: Plastic scrap—
  Recycling—Juvenile literature. | LCSH: Refuse as art material—Juvenile
  literature. | LCSH: Handicraft—Juvenile literature.
Classification: LCC TT297 .N45 2021 | DDC j745.57/2—dc23

Library of Congress Cataloging-in-Publication Data

Names: Nelson, Louise, author.
Title: Plastic eco activities / written by Louise Nelson.
Description: New York, NY : Crabtree Publishing Company, 2021. |
  Series: Eco activities | Includes index.
Identifiers: LCCN 2020045605 (print) | LCCN 2020045606 (ebook) |
  ISBN 9781427128621 (hardcover) |
  ISBN 9781427128669 (paperback) |
  ISBN 9781427128706 (ebook)
Subjects: LCSH: Plastics--Juvenile literature. | Plastics--Environmental aspects--
  Juvenile literterture. | Recycling industry--Juvenile literature. | Refuse and refuse
  disposal--Juvenile literature.
Classification: LCC TP1125 .N35 2021 (print) | LCC TP1125 (ebook) |
  DDC 668.4--dc23
LC record available at https://lccn.loc.gov/2020045605
LC ebook record available at https://lccn.loc.gov/2020045606

Crabtree Publishing Company

www.crabtreebooks.com   1-800-387-7650
Published by Crabtree Publishing Company in 2021

Printed in the U.S.A./122020/CG20201014

Published in Canada
Crabtree Publishing
616 Welland Avenue
St. Catharines, Ontario
L2M 5V6

Published in the United States
Crabtree Publishing
347 Fifth Ave
Suite 1402-145
New York, NY 10016

CONTENTS

Page 4   A Plastic Plan

Page 6   What Is Plastic?

Page 8   A Plastic Paradise

Page 12   A Plastic Posy

Page 16   Plastic Power!

Page 18   Plastic Planters

Page 22   Plastic Play!

Page 24   Glossary and Index

Words that are bolded can be found in the glossary on page 24.

A PLASTIC PLAN

STOP! Don't throw that plastic bottle in the garbage! That is really bad for the planet. There are a lot of things you could do with it instead.

Did you know?
Many of the things we throw away can be used again for something else.

Every minute, about a truck-full of plastic is thrown into the ocean. What can we do to stop this from happening?

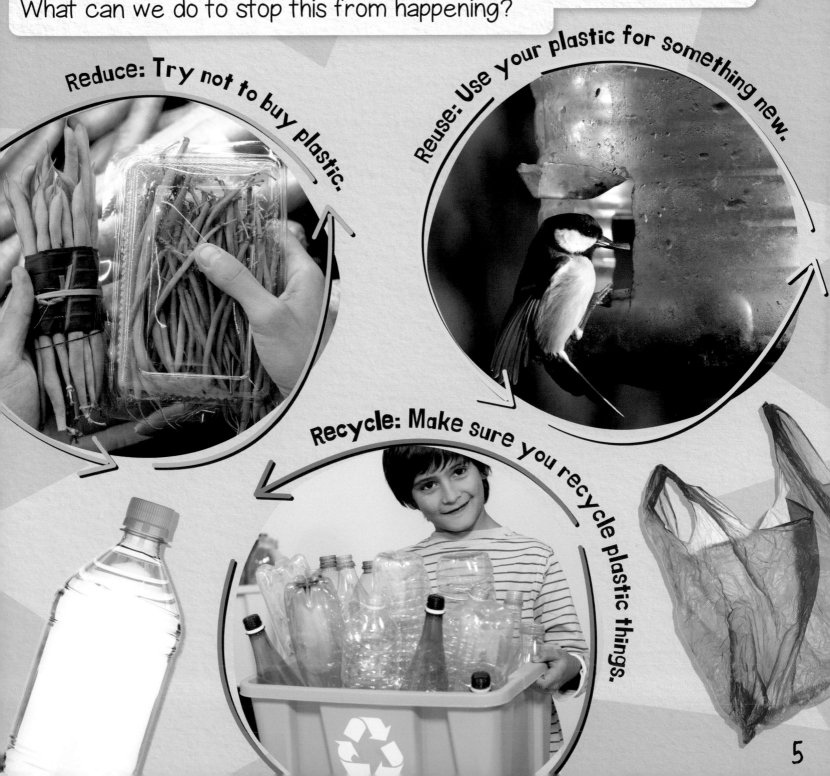

Reduce: Try not to buy plastic.

Reuse: Use your plastic for something new.

Recycle: Make sure you recycle plastic things.

WHAT IS PLASTIC?

Plastic is a material. We use materials, such as wood, glass, paper, and metal, to make things. Materials have properties. Properties tell us what the material is like.

The Properties of Plastic

Can be shaped into almost any shape

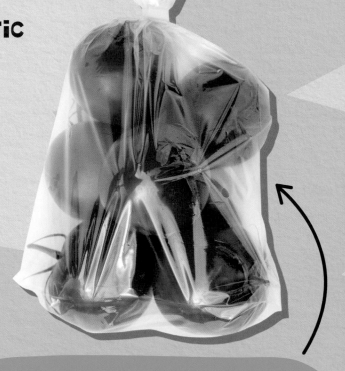

Can be thin and **transparent** (such as a plastic bag)

6

Can be thick and **opaque** (such as a lunchbox)

Made by people

Can last a long time— even hundreds of years!

A PLASTIC PARADISE

Let's keep that plastic out of the ocean. We can use it to make an ocean scene instead!

This works great as a class project. Can you fill a whole wall?

You will need:

- A lot of bottle caps in different colors
- Large piece of cardboard (an old cardboard box will work great)
- Plastic bottles in different colors
- String
- Googly eyes
- Paper and glue
- Markers
- Pipe cleaners
- Scissors
- Tape

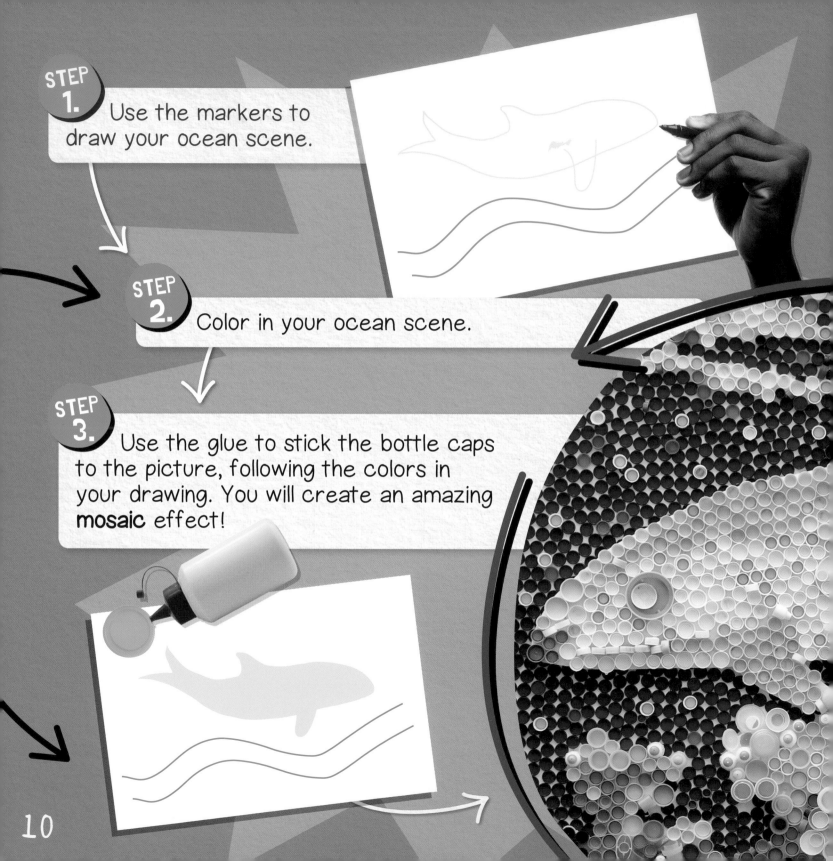

STEP 1. Use the markers to draw your ocean scene.

STEP 2. Color in your ocean scene.

STEP 3. Use the glue to stick the bottle caps to the picture, following the colors in your drawing. You will create an amazing **mosaic** effect!

STEP 4. Cut your colored plastic bottles to make fish.

STEP 5. Use pipe cleaners and bottle caps to make other sea creatures, like this crab! What other sea creatures can you make?

STEP 6. Hang your creatures in front of your colorful ocean scene.

A PLASTIC POSY

Make this lovely bunch of blooms for someone special or to brighten up a windowsill or garden!

If you want to recycle your flowers afterward, don't paint them. Use colored bottles instead.

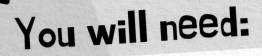

You will need:

- Plastic drink bottles (the kind with the bumps at the bottom)
- Acrylic paint
- Paintbrushes
- Thin wooden sticks (to use as stems)
- Felt or paper (for the leaves)
- Masking tape
- Aprons and newspaper
- Scissors

Clean as You Go

Don't forget to put newspaper down in your working area and wear an apron.

STEP 1. Ask an adult to cut around the bumpy edges of the bottom of the bottle, following the shape made by the bumps.

STEP 2. If you want to, paint inside each bump to look like colorful petals.

14

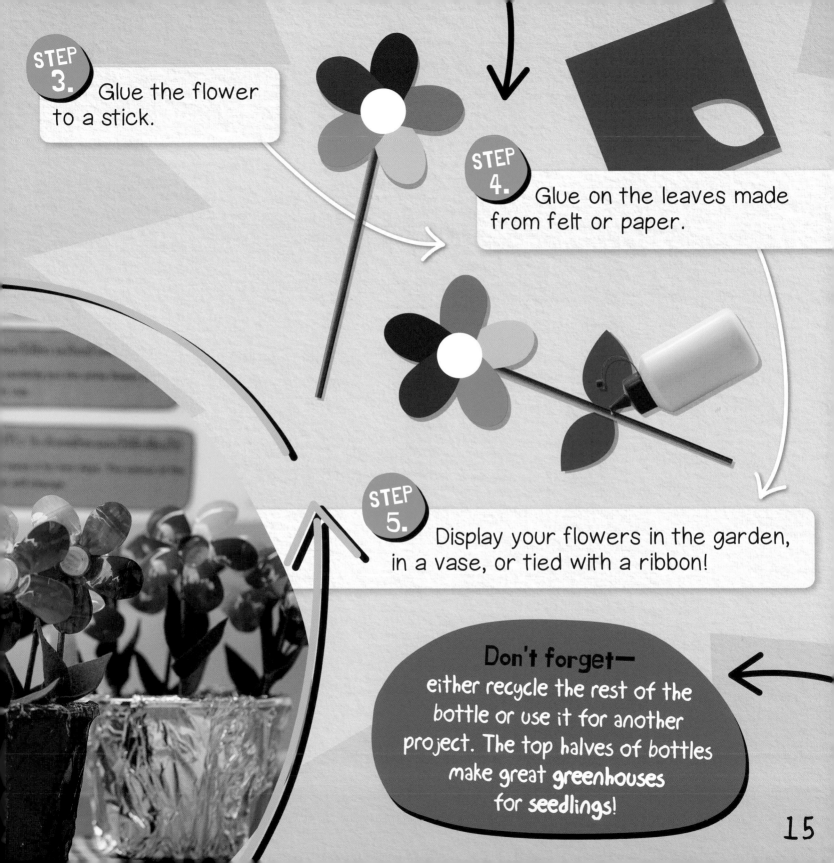

STEP 3. Glue the flower to a stick.

STEP 4. Glue on the leaves made from felt or paper.

STEP 5. Display your flowers in the garden, in a vase, or tied with a ribbon!

Don't forget— either recycle the rest of the bottle or use it for another project. The top halves of bottles make great **greenhouses** for **seedlings!**

15

PLASTIC POWER!

Plastic that isn't reused or recycled can end up in the oceans. Plastic bags can look like food to hungry turtles, and other trash can float around in the water for a long time, **polluting** the water.

When we throw away plastic, it is important to make sure that we do it in the right way.

There are some simple steps to take that can help! When you are done with a plastic item, wash it carefully. Check the label to see which parts of the item can be recycled. Put each part in the right bin.

PLASTIC PLANTERS

These adorable kitty planters will brighten up any windowsill!
Plastic is a good material for plant pots because it is **waterproof**.

Plastics in the ocean can break down into tiny pieces, called microplastics. Microplastics are small enough to get into the bodies of birds and fish.

You will need:

- Plastic bottles
- Acrylic paint
- Beads, stickers, and gems
- Permanent markers
- Stones
- A plant in a pot
- Water

Don't Forget!

Permanent markers will stain anything they touch. Put the lids back on as soon as you are done with them.

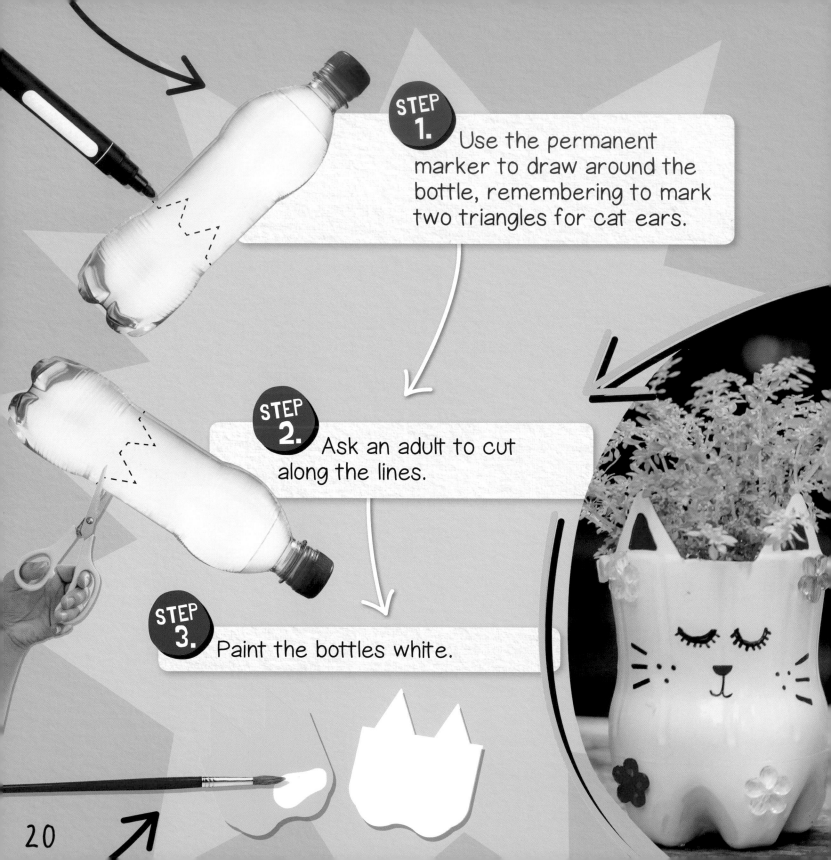

STEP 1. Use the permanent marker to draw around the bottle, remembering to mark two triangles for cat ears.

STEP 2. Ask an adult to cut along the lines.

STEP 3. Paint the bottles white.

STEP 4. Use the markers to draw on a kitty face.

STEP 5. Decorate your planter with beads, gems, or stickers.

STEP 6. Put a handful of stones in the bottom of the pot to add weight.

STEP 7. Put your plant (and its pot) into the planter.

Don't forget to give your plant a little drink of water too!

PLASTIC PLAY!

These games are simple to make with paper, crayons, and bottle caps.

Bottle-cap Bingo!

Draw circles on a piece of paper. Color them in different colors. Put different colored bottle caps into a bag. Now, take turns picking out a bottle cap. If it matches a colored circle on your paper, place it on that circle. The first one to fill their piece of paper wins.

Tic-tac-toe

Write X's and O's on bottle caps and make a travel tic-tac-toe game!

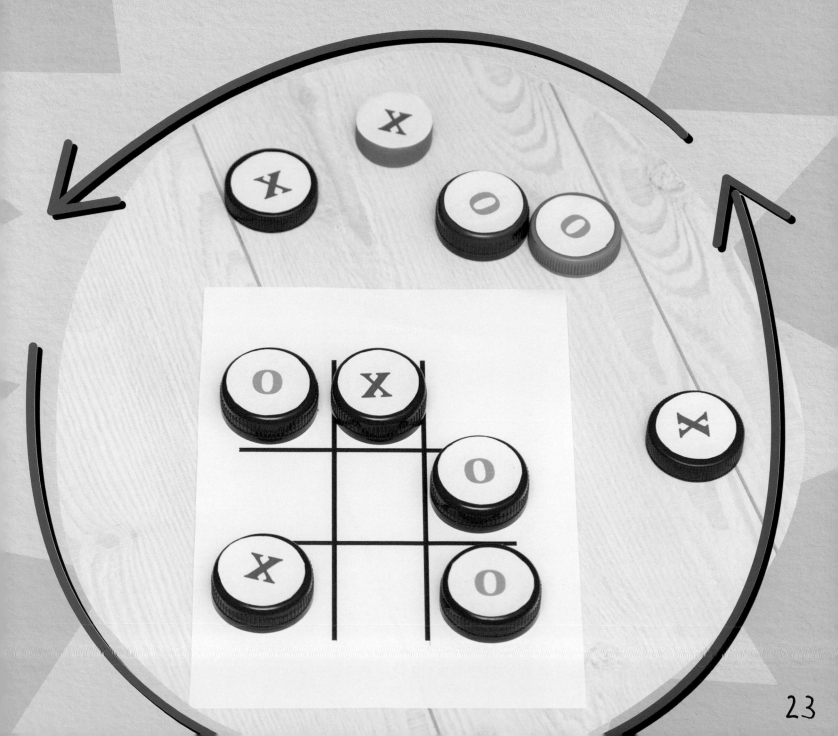

GLOSSARY

greenhouses	Glass buildings that are used for growing plants in
mosaic	Pictures or patterns that are created by putting together small pieces of stone, tile, or glass
opaque	Not see-through
polluting	When something harmful or poisonous is added to the natural world
recycle	Use again to make something else
seedlings	Young plants
transparent	See-through
waterproof	Stops water from getting through

INDEX

bags 6, 16, 22

bottle caps 9–11, 22–23

bottles 4, 9, 11–15, 19–20

games 22–23

materials 6, 18

oceans 5, 8, 10, 16, 18

plants 15, 19, 21

properties 6–7

water 16, 18–19, 21